Couples Guide

Charles R. Swindoll
with John D. Sloan

MULTNOMAH PRESS

PORTLAND, OREGON 97266

Other books by Charles R. Swindoll
You and Your Child
For Those Who Hurt
Second Wind: A Fresh Run at Life
Hand Me Another Brick
Killing Giants, Pulling Thorns
Home: Where Life Makes Up Its Mind
Three Steps Forward, Two Steps Back

All Scripture references are from the New American Standard Bible,
© the Lockman Foundation 1960, 1962, 1963, 1968, 1971, 1972, 1973,
1975, 1977, and are used by permission.

Book photography and design by Paul Lewis

© 1980 by Multnomah Press
Portland, Oregon 97266

Second printing 1980
Printed in the United States of America

ISBN 0-930014-49-9

CONTENTS

INTRODUCTION

The American family is in trouble. One authority on marriage has said that our society has reached the point where happily married couples seem to be an "oddity." Even though some form of the family has been found in every known society, one anthropologist has now demanded a substitute for the family unit. Frederick Engles, most widely known as one of the creators of modern communism, made a similar demand over a century ago. It has been estimated that some 20 million American couples live in desperate unhappiness and unfulfillment. The number increases every year.

This sad scene has also affected Christian marriages. And there is a desperate need to right this devastating trend with the power and knowledge that God has made available.

We need to get back to the basics. Who designed the home anyway? Since God brought forth this human relationship, what does He consider to be essential in marriage? How has He planned for marriage not only to survive, but also to be genuinely fulfilling and satisfying?

The Aim

The aim of this couple's guide is to explore the ground that has been broken in the book *Strike the Original Match*. It is designed to enable every couple to discuss and answer those questions in the preceeding paragraph. This guide will also help a group of couples gather together to talk about the essentials of marriage, and then relate how marriage can survive and even thrive in today's society—all from a biblical perspective.

6   What's In the Guide?

This booklet will aid the leader who invites a group of couples to study the book *Strike the Original Match* together. But it is best if each couple in the group has a guide along with the book itself. The guide has twelve studies to coordinate with the twelve main chapters of the book. Each assignment is divided into four areas. There is a section on the purpose of the assignment, a section expressly devoted to the study of Scripture, a section labeled *Thought Questions* which are exactly that, and a final section called *Putting It Into Practice* which will help a couple apply the study to their lives.

A *Scripture Index* and a *Subject Index* for the book *Strike the Original Match* are also provided in the back of the guide to help those who wish to dig deeper and research the scriptures mentioned in the book. The *Scripture Index* gives a listing of every verse that is used and the page of the book on which it is used. Use the *Subject Index* to quickly locate the author's view on key issues and topics.

Where Do We Meet?

Ideally, this can be a three-month study for a group of interested couples. It would be preferable for the gathering to be a once-a-week affair in a non-threatening setting such as the home. At least six people are needed to reduce the tenseness that probably crops up in a small group, but as many as eight couples can participate effectively. Just remember—the larger the group the more readily the information can be gathered, but the less deeply the issues can be pursued.

Who Should We Invite?

The big question about one of these fellowship gatherings is always, "Who do we invite?" If you want a group composed of married couples, ask people with common interests, who are about the same age. Or, as a pastor, you may wish to gather engaged couples together in a group fashion with this study as the focus. A pastor might even want to gather couples together who need marriage counseling. Possibly a study could be made up of engaged couples formed out of a college fellowship group. Whether couples are about ready to get married or about ready to celebrate 25 years of married life, this study can be used effectively to rekindle and build that marriage flame!

What Is Expected of Us?

In approaching the assignments in the couple's guide, a person should remember that the assignment schedule is coordinated with the chapters in the book. The designated chapter needs to be read in the book before tackling the couple's guide. Then a couple needs to read through the *Purposes* section in the guide, and individually (or together) work through the *Scripture Input*. The *Thought Questions* in the couple's guide apply to families as well as couples, so take time at the dinner table to discuss one thought question per day. Make an effort to implement the action step as it applies to the couples' group or your home, or both! When you return to the study each week, you'll have plenty of questions, reports, and suggestions to discuss and share.

How Do We Begin?

Getting started is an exciting time in such a group study. When you talk to couples about participation in the study, ask them to be willing to invest the time for the study and the money for the book and guide. Commitment at the front end of the study is always best. And if couples will agree to this, you can purchase the books and guides and have them available at the first meeting. That is much better than having staggered purchases of the materials throughout the life of the small-group project.

Explain the purpose of the study at the first meeting. Show the couples the format of the guide, and how that format should be followed at home as well as in the weekly discussion study. Be sure to maintain this format at each weekly meeting. You will experience a strong temptation to jump to the final section and share how the week went with the spouse and family. Don't yield to that urge! Go through the *Purpose*, the *Scripture Input*, and the *Thought Questions* first. In the end you will be pleased you stayed with this methodical game plan. So will those in the group.

Time is crucial in a study such as this. Plan for at least one hour of unhindered interaction time with the couple's guide material. You may want to plan and enjoy about a half hour of refreshments and "milling" before you start your group discussion. This is especially true for the first session. Concerning time for each of the assignments, the leader

8   should ask for about two hours of discussing and reading outside the weekly session time. That's only about 3% of a couple's available time in a week after work, rest, and meals. And your marriage is certainly worthy of the investment!

Anything to Be Careful of?

A few comments need to be made about personality tendencies of individuals that can hinder the progress of the group. Occasionally, there is the attitude of domination—the "Bull Moose" tendency of controlling the discussion either for the sake of flattery or because of a "know-it-all" complex. Another destructive attitude as far as possible group interaction goes is that of playfulness—a little light-heartedness certainly helps to break the ice in any situation, but continual side-tracking by "Mr. Tom Foolery" through jokes and puns about every statement can only prove distracting and irritating. On the other side of the scale, the "Sad Sack" approach that comes from the "it-will-never-work" pessimist or the easily offended pouter is equally destructive to group progress. Finally, the seemingly unharmful approach of "standing in the wings" or looking on without comment is not healthy in a group discussion.

It would be good to talk about these unhelpful attitudes graciously and honesty at the first study. Frankly, all of us have one or more of these tendencies. As you discuss these attitudes, talk about ways to 1) encourage participation by all the group, 2) stay on the subject at hand, 3) allow and appreciate times of silence by the group for thought, 4) create an atmosphere where couples are free to share and free to fail, and 5) guard against embarrassing anyone for any reason.

One more thing. In most groups there will probably be the need for a baby-sitter. Why not talk about getting one or two people to be sitters for the entire group of children? Share the expense between couples. Then, when the 12-week study is over, honor the person or persons who have served you in this way. Sponsor one couple from your group to treat the person(s) who did the babysitting to a special evening.

Enough of rules and guidelines. Let's dig in and see what God has to say about marriage!

And before plunging in—why not pray? Pray specifically 9
that God will make each study meaningful and encouraging.

LET'S CONSULT THE ARCHITECT

Purposes

To get a good look at the original marriage.

To be made aware of 4 steps that we can take in our own marriage to make it strong.

To examine the 3 essential qualities you will need as a couple in order to make the 4 steps work.

Scripture Input

Read Genesis 1:12,18, 21, and 31, 2:18-25; Psalm 127:1; Proverbs 2:6, 24:3-4.

1. In comparing the verse in Genesis 2:18 with the verses of Genesis 1:12,18,21, and 31, you will note that a list of positive statements are counteracted by a negative statement. What was God's reason for saying, ". . . it is *not* good"?

2. How did God remedy Adam's "isolation" problem in Genesis 2:18? What do the words "a helper suitable for him" mean from a husband's perspective? From a wife's perspective? Be specific.

3. They say that a dog is a man's best friend. What does Genesis 2:19-20 say about that statement? Discuss the unique meaning of the words "a helper suitable for him."

4. Look at Genesis 2:21-25. How did the creation of woman differ from the creation of other animal life? God didn't create woman from dust as He did man, either. Does that say anything to you about the uniqueness of woman?

12
   5. What does Adam's reaction in verse 23 (in *The Living Bible*) tell you about the Designer's foresight of Adam's explicit needs in a wife? Do you share in this thought about your husband or wife? Why or why not?

   6. Adam was whipped into shape from dust. Eve's physical structure was formed from bone and sinew—Adam's bone and sinew. Is the difference in origin significant? Since you and your mate have differences in make-up and attitudes, does this passage say anything to you? List the differences you do have—everything from personality to tastes, from talents to eating habits. Talk through the importance of these differences to your marriage.

   7. What 4 guidelines for a meaningful marriage are found in Genesis 2:24-25? These will be discussed in the next chapter, but stop and talk about these principles now. Using each portion of Scripture like ". . . a man shall leave his father and mother" as a guide, paraphrase the 4 principles in your own words.

   8. Look closely at the words of Proverbs 24:3-4:
> *By wisdom a house is "built,"*
> *And by understanding it is "established";*
> *And by knowledge the rooms are "filled"*
> *With all precious and pleasant riches.*

Concentrate on the actions suggested by the verbs. Now note the objects of these action verbs. What do these verbs suggest as the primary "construction" activity of any couple who own their own home?

   9. Look up the following verses in relation to the topics, Wisdom, Understanding and Knowledge—Proverbs 1:5-7, 2:1-11, 3:13-26, 4:4-12, 7:2-4, 8:1-12, 9:1-12, 10:13-14, 13:14-16, 16:21-24, 19:8, 22:17-21. What are the differences in meaning of these 3 terms? How do these qualities apply to your marriage and home? Are they being hindered in their use at your house? If so, how?

   10. Read Psalm 127 together. Discuss ways these words are becoming a reality in your home. Try to be specific.

Thought Questions 13

11. Imagine for a moment that God did not bring you "a suitable helper." How would this affect your life today? Discuss the differences it would make in your family if the helper had been "unsuitable."

12. Using Genesis 2:21-23 as a basis for discussion, share with your partner and your family the unique qualities you see in him or her. Let each family member add to the list. Take these responses and use them as short "thankfuls" during table blessings this week. (Be careful! Some of the positive statements that leak out from these meetings could startle your neighbors!)

13. Make a list of all the things that you value in your home, from stereos to workshops, from sewing machines to picture frames. If your house was destroyed, what "valuables" would remain from your home? Think honestly: "How much emphasis do I place on *things* in our home?"

Putting It Into Practice

Discuss the essentials of the perfect home from a biblical viewpoint. Construct a "group exchange" where ideas from each group member are noted on a blackboard or overhead transparency. Act and react about how reforms or reinforcements can bring about needed changes in your imperfect home. On your own as a couple, try hard to affirm your love for one another as you deal honestly with the reality of things as they are in your home.

LET'S
REPAIR
THE
FOUNDATION

Purpose

To delve into the 4 marriage-strengthening principles of Severance, Permanence, Unity, and Intimacy.

Scripture Input

Read Genesis 2:24-25, 3:9-10; Matthew 19:4-6; 1 Corinthians 7:3-4; and Ephesians 5:22-23.

1. Read the account of the actor's response to the question "What make a great lover?" (*Strike the Original Match*, page 27) Share your initial feelings about his statements in light of current popular opinion about alternatives and "temporariness" in marriages today. What does the Bible say on this subject?

2. Meditate on the following clause:
"For this cause a man shall leave his father and his mother..."
What is the context—that is, the biblical words and sentences surrounding the verses—of this statment? Does marriage signify a "break from the past"? In what ways? Read Ephesians 6:1-3 and discuss how the principles of severance and respect of parents can be retained when two people leave their families and establish a new home.

3. Think about severance from the perspective of a parent. How can a parent help to effect this principle? How can a parent hinder the home-leaving process?

4. Add on the next part of this verse:
"For this cause a man shall leave his father and his mother, and shall cleave to his wife ..."

16 As you think about the verb *cleave*, remember that it means to "cling," or "adhere to." Keep this in mind as you look at the following passages:

2 Kings 5:27 – leprosy "clings" to one's body

Job 19:20 – bones "cling" to skin (in the case of an emaciated, diseased person)

Jeremiah 13:11 – a waistband or belt "clings" to the waist of a man (in order to tightly restrain or hold firmly out of the way a person's tunic so that free movement is allowed)

The sensation you should get from studying this verb is that a tight, close, firm-holding action is being described. Apply this to the marriage bond. What does it say about a man's and woman's marriage union? What does it indicate about God's view of this bond?

5. Jesus referred back to this main passage on marriage (Genesis 2:24-25) when questioned by an intimidating group of religionists about divorce. Read Matthew 19:4-5 slowly. Now look at Jesus's statement in verse 6, especially the last clause. What was Christ's view of the permanence of marriage? According to Christ, who actually consummates the union? Does this give you a new view as to why a breaking of this permanent bond is so unbiblical? Explain your answer.

6. Study the next phrase of Genesis 2:24.

"... and they shall become one flesh."

We are looking at the principle of *unity* here. Do the words "shall become" indicate a process or an instantaneous fact? What advantage is there in seeing marriage as a continuing series of steps toward a goal rather than a "once and for all" accomplishment at the altar? Has anyone reading this guide ever "arrived" as far as marriage is concerned? Briefly discuss a couple or three processes you are currently working through.

7. There are some telling words recorded in I Corinthians 7:3-4 about unity in marriage. Verse 4 states that a husband has full authority and freedom over his wife's body in respect to marital affairs. Verse 4 also states that a wife has full authority or freedom over her husband's body in the same way. How can this be accomplished? What personality tendencies could get in the way of such an unselfish arrangement? Is this type of unity described elsewhere in the Bible?

8. Intimacy is a delicate subject. Genesis 2:25 is a biblical description of tender intimacy in marriage. Honor and beauty describes the marriage bed rather than shame and disgust. Obtain a copy of *The Living Bible*. As husband and wife, read the account of the Song of Solomon to one another, the husband reading the part of King Solomon and the wife reading the part of the woman. What does this biblical book teach you about openness and intimacy in marriage? (For a more descriptive and elaborate study of this biblical book, read Craig Glickman's *A Song for Lover's*, an InterVarsity Press publication.)

Thought Questions

9. A good exercise that tests your family's spiritual barometer is to take Ephesians 5:15-21 and talk about it at the dinner table. Are these things true in your family unit? Is there harmony, gratitude, and humility being demonstrated between family members?

10. Hold a family "panel discussion" and talk about the *severance* principle. Discuss the pros and cons of leaving the "nest" too quickly or not quickly enough. Now, switch roles in the discussion, the parents representing the side of the children and the children the parents' role. Make plans for this future event in your family's life. Talk about how that process can begin now and continue for several years.

11. Think about your commitment to each other, as family members and as spouses. How long has it been since you have *verbally* declared that to one another? Is it time to have an "eyeball-to-eyeball" commitment talk with one of the family members . . . alone with each other and in a place you won't be interrupted?

Putting It Into Practice

Using the 4 guidelines of Severance, Permanence, Unity, and Intimacy as measurements of marital success, take a poll of marriage partners at the office, store, shop, etc., to see which of these principles have been put into practice. Take stock of your own marriage. Does the absence of any one of these necessitate certain repair measures in your own home? When can these repairs start taking place?

BRICKS THAT BUILD A MARRIAGE

Purposes

To discover and put to use the practical building materials for healthy marriages that are found in the Bible.

Scripture Input

Read aloud Proverbs 31:10-31; Ephesians 5:22-23; I Timothy 3:4-5; and I Peter 3:1-9.

1. We will refer to Ephesians 5:22-23 again in this study. Place it in front of you in several different translations if possible. What is the extended comparison that is used in this analogy? God is described as the bridegroom and His people as His bride elsewhere in the Bible. Read Ezekiel 16:8-14 for the analogy of God as the bridegroom and the people of Israel as the bride. What is significant about these comparisons? Do they say anything to you about God's concept of marriage?

2. God thinks highly of the relationship called marriage. In fact, He thinks so much of marriage that He compares the husband-wife relationship to the relationship of Christ to the church. As you think about the church's relationship to Christ, wives, what attitudes are most important for the church to demonstrate to her Savior? Does this carry over into your marriage? What attitudes did Christ display toward the church, husbands? Is this being demonstrated in your marriage?

3. Carefully construct the biblical definition of submission. Take your time. Choose your wording wisely. Is this

20   understood in today's culture? Define sacrificial love according to Ephesians 5:25. Do most Christian husbands you know show an understanding of this concept? Why or why not?

4. Read I Peter 3:1-2. What is the "belief-instilling" instrument God uses on a husband from the life of a submissive wife? How can a woman's actions be the most powerful evangelism tool in a home?

5. A contrast is set up between verses 3 and 4 of Peter's third chapter. Two types of adornment are described – inner and outer. Does this section dictate dark, morbid attire for all godly women? Or does it suggest a doormat type of attitude for women who aspire to have imperishable qualities God deems precious?

6. A gentle and quiet woman, that is, one who has a dignified self-control and a tranquil attitude that radiates confidence and assurance, is described in Proverbs 31:10-31. Is this picture of a godly woman familiar to you? If not, read about her in this passage of Scripture. Look for similar situations in your home's life style that would allow for such a display of virtue.

7. "Thus Sarah *obeyed* Abraham . . ." This same verb is used in Hebrews 5:9. What is the result there?

8. In I Peter 3:6, the wife's response of obedience brings forth belief in the husband's life, too. How do you feel about the response of obedience, wives? Is there an assurance that you won't be exploited for your submissive response? Where? But what about that wife you know who is being taken advantage of by her husband?

9. Passivity in male leadership has diseased Christian homes everywhere. Yet church leadership demands good home managers for its office holders (cf. I Timothy 3:4-5). In what ways does I Peter 3:7 address this subject?

10. Patient understanding is a virtue of the godly husband according to I Peter 3:7. Think specifically of the times *this* week you have neglected to sit down with your wife after work and listen to her day's problems. What took the time she really deserves?

11. A wife is called a "fellow heir" of God's grace. Strong
words! What do they mean? Is there any penalty for not giving
this honor to your wife, husbands?

12. As a couple, employ the 4 suggestions given at the
end of Chapter 3 in *Strike the Original Match* (p. 53). Be ready
to share the results at the weekly group meeting.

Thought Questions

13. Can you think of a woman in your past who literally
fulfilled the I Peter 3 role of a wife? How did she affect those
around her, especially her husband? How did she affect you?

14. Do the same as you did in question 1 in thinking
about Peter's conception of a husband. Husbands, share un-
guarded reactions and feelings about such a model for a male.
(If you think this person only exists in superman storybooks,
say so! But be ready to listen to examples of men who are
actually filling this role–empowered by the Holy Spirit.)

15. Meditate on I Peter 3:8-9 as a family. Think of family
situations where these qualities do or don't exist. Then talk
about bringing them into reality. Deal specifically with each
quality, one by one.

Putting It Into Practice

Each day this week, read Ephesians 5:22-33 to one
another–first the wife's portion (5:22-24, 33b) and then the
husband's (5:25-33a). Each time reference is made to a wife
or husband, insert your own first name. Ask God to make
these attitudes real in your actions toward your mate this
week. Pray with one another, asking God to assist you in ac-
complishing this desire.

WATCH OUT FOR CHEAP SUBSTITUTES!

Purpose

To be made aware of the inferior building materials some couples settle for as they hammer out their own marriage design in place of God's.

Scripture Input

Read Genesis 27 and I Peter 3:1-9.

1. "What you see is what you don't get!"
That should be the label on much of the synthetic and artificial merchandise that is peddled in stores as a replacement for the real thing. From flowers to fabrics, the purpose is to fool. Talk about some of the synthetics and substitutes that are found in every store. List what imitations can and cannot do. Now apply these thoughts to the use of cheap substitutes in marriage rather than genuine qualities of godly character.

> NOTE: In these next questions, you will be using Scripture as the source of the positive actions for marital success while examining the substitutes that some couples use.

2. As you read I Peter 3:1-2, underline the words *won without a word*. Secret manipulation (winning another over by unfair means) is cited as a substitute used by some wives to win their way. God says win by behavior – man says master by manipulation. Think about some common manipulative techniques. Turn to Proverbs 3:3-8. What are the benefits of truthful, straightforward dealing? What are the advantages of doing things God's way?

24   3. A clear biblical example for secret manipulation by a wife is found in Genesis 27. Read about Rebekah's secret maneuvering with her favorite son, Jacob. Are there lessons to be learned from this story? (Not only was there animosity between Esau's people, the Edomites, and Jacob's people, the Israelites, during the remainder of biblical history, but Jacob was the victim of deceit and scheming in chapter 29—proof positive that deceit breeds deceit!) Be honest, now. Can you recall an occasion when you used manipulation to get what you wanted?

4. Type out the words of I Peter 3:3-4 on an index card, and tape it to the mirror in your bathroom. This exercise is to remind you of the danger of concentrating too much attention on external beauty. Consider the time you spend in front of the mirror each day. Is there too much time being spent here daily? What inner beauty preparations could use some of that overtime in front of the mirror? Can you name an inner-beauty trait you really need to develop?

5. There is an emphasis on "doing" what is right in I Peter 3:6. Ladies, list the major activities that you do each week. How many of these activities relate to your husbands and families? Do you need to reevaluate your schedule?

6. Again our passage is I Peter 3:7. The substitute that masquerades as the breadwinner complex takes hold of many a husband after marriage newness wears off. Read I Corinthians 13:4-7 aloud and slowly. List the number of times providing a living is listed as a characteristic of Christlike love. Is there more to love than insurance policies? Name some specific ways your love could be better demonstrated.

7. The wife is described as the "weaker vessel" in this section of Scripture. This distinction of weakness can be appreciated by comparing your finest china to your rugged cast-iron skillets. Hence, delicate fragility rather than inferior quality is being stressed. Think about that. Are there advantages in understanding your wife's "weaknesses"? Are her physical limitations appreciated at your house or is she put under pressure because of them?

8. Intimidation is a tactic used by some husbands to manage their wife and family. What are some examples of intimidation? What light does I Peter 3:7 shed on this subject?

9. Another unbiblical attitude for the husband who uses substitutes is the tendency towards smothering instead of honoring "as a fellow heir of the grace of life." Look up Galatians 3:28, a verse that refers to every Christian's standing before Christ. Although the roles of man and woman are different in a marriage, what is the same as far as one's relationship to Christ? Do certain leadership styles of Christian husbands deny this reality? How? What part does uncontrolled jealousy play in the use of this substitute? What is the cure for domination or smothering? How could a change be effected?

10. I Peter 3:8-9 sums up the attitudes that combat cheap substitutism.

"To sum up, let all be harmonious, sympathetic, brotherly, kindhearted, and humble in spirit; not returning evil for evil, or insult for insult, but giving a blessing instead; for you were called for the very purpose that you might inherit a blessing."

Now take these verses, and do the following exercise. Turn all the positive statements into negative ones. For example, write "let all be *un*harmonious, . . .returning insult for insult," etc.

Before you exclaim how horrible this twisted verson is, look at your own home. Honestly, does your home resemble this type of selfish behavior more often than not? On a scale of 1 to 10 (1 being most of the time and 10 being very rarely), rate your marriage and family life as to how often the biblical version of I Peter 3:8-9 is a reality. What specific steps could you take to improve this rating? Are you willing to trust God to bring about these changes, painful though they may be? Pray seriously about *one* major factor that currently hinders the change. Ask Him to remove it.

Thought Questions

11. Review the 3 substitutes wives often use to cover up what's missing in their marriage. Contrast these with the 4 bricks of chapter 3 that wives are advised to use. As a wife, how do you feel about your building in these areas? As a husband, how do you feel about your spouse in this regard?

12. Review the husband's substitutes and the real bricks he should be using. As a husband, how do you measure up? As a wife, how do you feel about your spouse?

26   Putting It Into Practice

Take some time to think about your goals as a couple. What can you change as a wife, as a husband, to make those goals come true? What substitutes need to be replaced in your marriage? Have a blab session in your group this week. Brainstorm and come up with concrete steps that can be taken to eliminate the cheap substitutes from your marriages and achieve the biblical goals you have as a couple.

5

WHO SAYS THE HONEYMOON MUST END?

Purpose

To explore the ways in which a couple can develop a fulfilling, mutual intimate relationship so that meaningful romance and a sexual desire will never lose its edge.

Scripture Input

Read Genesis 1:27-31; Proverbs 5:1-15, 15-21; Song of Solomon 5:10-15, 7:1-10; 1 Corinthians 7:1-5; Hebrews 13:4.

1. What are some of the common misconceptions about honeymoons? (For example, that there are no differences of opinion during this time, that sex is always an enjoyable experience right from the start, etc.)

2. Are there advantages to seeing the honeymoon as an adjustment period rather than a romantic dream with no flaw? Would this have helped you before marriage? Were there some "honeymoon hangups" that have seriously impacted your sexual relationship today?

3. In conjunction with the reading of Genesis 1:27-31, note the declaration "it was very good." To what may this declaration be applied in the preceding verses? Does this statement apply to the command, "Be fruitful and multiply. . . ." (vv. 22, 28) What, then, is *God's* opinion about sex?

4. Turning to the pages of the New Testament, we see that God's original blessing upon marital intimacy did not change.

"Let marriage be held in honor among all, and let the marriage bed be undefiled; . . ." Hebrews 13:4

28   Literally, the first of that verse reads:

"Marriage is honorable in all."

In order to get an idea of the "precious value" God attaches to the marriage relationship and all that goes with it—including sex—let's examine His use of that word "honorable." Look up the following verses: 1 Corinthians 3:12; James 5:7; 1 Peter 1:7,19; 2 Peter 1:4; Revelation 17:4, 18:12,16, 21:11,19. Keep in mind that the word translated "precious, very costly" is the same word translated "honorable" in Hebrews 13:4.

What else does this adjective describe besides the marriage union? Does the fact that God places the same value on marriage that He does on priceless gems, the rich promises of the Word, and even the invaluable blood of His own Son affect your concept of marriage? Of marital intimacy?

5.   Is sex only intended for procreation and propagation of the human species? Read Proverbs 5:15-19. Answer this question with more than a "yes" or "no."

6.   Take a copy of *The Living Bible*, and read Song of Solomon 5:10-15 and 7:1-10. The first passage is a speech about his wife. Does the presence of such passages in the Bible add to the emphasis that has been made about God's high view of sex? What can each spouse learn about display of affection within marriage from these verses? (Read 1:8-9, 2:3-6, 4:1-15, and 6:4-9 as well) Is communication an important part of marital intimacy? Are you and your spouse free to communicate about these things?

7.   Study 1 Corinthians 7:1-2. Is our society a believer of this principle?

8.   What are the consequences of sex outside and prior to marriage? Some biblical passages that pertain to this subject include Proverbs 5:1-6, 6:20-35, and 7:1-27. Think about the "reversal of roles" mentioned on page 77 in the fifth chapter of *Strike the Original Match*.

9.   We have cited 1 Corinthians 7:2-3 as keystone verses for the principle of unselfish affection being a part of intimacy within marriage. Look up the following verses to build your backlog of truth about the principle of being unselfish: Romans 12:10; 1 Corinthians 10:24, 13:5; 2 Corinthians 5:15; Philippians 2:3-4; James 2:8.

10. Can a correlation be drawn between moral failures in Christian marriages and the lack of strong sexual relationships in those same marriages? What does 1 Corinthians 7:5 contribute to your thoughts here?

Thought Questions

11. Think back to the honeymoon that you took as a couple after you were first married. What made it so special? What attitudes did you have that contributed to the enjoyment of those first days together? Which of those attitudes are still in operation today?

12. Take some of the passages from the Song of Solomon that we studied and write them down on paper. From the wife's standpoint, what is appreciated about the husband's words to the wife? From the husband's standpoint, what does he appreciate about the wife's words to her husband? Verbalize some of your own creative compliments to your mate using this Scripture for a guide.

13. Some say marriage is a "50-50" proposition. What would happen, however, if each mate gave 100% to the other?

14. Think about Cliff Barrow's suggestion of maintaining marital harmony by the use of these 4 phrases: "I am wrong," "I am sorry," "Please forgive me," and "I love you." Would that solve a situation of disagreement you're facing with your mate today, and keep the honeymoon going?

Putting It Into Practice

Construct an imaginary interview in which a family member or couples' group member questions you during the first week of your marriage. Have the interviewer draw up a list of questions about your view of marriage during those first honeymooning days. Use this dramatization to spark a discussion about how your ideas of marriage have or have not changed.

A Special Creative Project: Want to try something *really* unique? Write a *very* intimate love note to your mate—much like the ones you read in Song of Solomon. Spell out your affection, the things you really adore about your partner.

30 Don't be afraid to tell it like it is (Solomon wasn't!). For an added surprise, tuck it under his/her pillow . . . or mail it to him/her. But be sure and put *personal* on the envelope. Nothing like having one of your kids rip open that love letter and read it at the supper table!

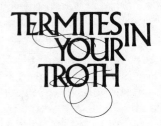

6

TERMITES IN YOUR TROTH

Purpose

To discuss the "little" problems that can weaken the marriage relationship from the inside like termites can weaken the foundation and internal structure of a house.

Scripture Input

Read Song of Solomon 2:15 and Ephesians 5:15-21.

1. As you read Song of Solomon 2:15, replace the word "foxes" with "termites" and the word "vineyards" with "marriage." Can you think of any "little" things that are eating away at your marriage relationship?

2. Turn to Psalm 139:23,24. Again, replace the words "hurtful way" with "termites." What admonition surfaces when you rephrase the verses in this manner? How does that relate to marriage?

3. Let's look closely at each of the termites spoken of in *Strike the Original Match.* The warning in Ephesians 5:15 is to "be careful how you walk." Don't be confused about your role as a husband or wife. Can you recall the material we have studied that gives clear and unconfused input about our roles in marriage? (Here's a hint to help you remember – the biblical books of Genesis, Proverbs, Song of Solomon, 1 Corinthians, and Ephesians are noteworthy places to start.)

4. There are 3 sources of marital confusion cited in *Strike the Original Match.* Beginning on page 89, the following befuddlers are cited: anti-marriage propaganda in our society, demands on parents' time and efforts because of the number of relationships in a family, and immaturity on the

32   part of the parents. Match the following verses with the appropriate problem mentioned above: Colossians 3:12-14; Ephesians 5:15-16 and Galatians 6:2; Proverbs 2:6-15.

5. Another of the termites that infects the homebuilding process is the one labeled *busyness*. Doing too many things—even though they are good things—in the hours that each of us are allotted. It would be good to get God's perspective on the use of time. Turn to Psalm 90 and slowly meditate on the words. What new things did you learn about time? Who does the writer suggest we can turn to for direction in our time management? Why?

6. "Workaholic" is a descriptive term for the plight of many men and women today. Does God say that work is not good? Read Luke 10:7; Ephesians 4:28; 1 Thessalonians 4:11-12. But is work "for the sake of work alone" good? Before you answer that question, read the thoughts of a man who discussed the subject of work for the sake of work alone—Ecclesiastes 2:18-23. If you are a high-achiever, better read these words again.

7. There is a balance between work and rest, a balance which even the Son of God recognized in His ministry on earth. In Mark 6:7-12, the disciples were sent out in pairs to minister. Upon their return, what did Jesus instruct them to do? Read Mark 6:30-32. What principles might we apply to our own lives from this?

8. The word "foolish" in Ephesians 5:17 can be interpreted to mean a lack of common-sense perception or a want of reason. The cure for a lack of common sense, the lack which can become an insensitivity to God and man (the third termite), is to know the will of the Lord. See what the following verses teach about the will of God: Romans 12:2, Ephesians 6:5,6; Colossians 1:9,10; 1 Thessalonians 4:3; Hebrews 13:21; 1 Peter 2:15. How can this knowledge counteract the third termite?

9. Stubbornness. Every red-blooded American has this characteristic to some degree. Mixed with a little rugged independence, it becomes some of the grit which forms the backbone of our country. But that same stick-to-your-guns attitude can become lethal in marriage. Meditate on this phrase:

"be subject to one another in the fear of Christ."
What does that phrase tell us about an independent spirit in marriage?

10 The verb used in Ephesians 5:21 means to put one-self under the authority of another. When neither husband nor wife wants to give in during the heat of a disagreement, how would this verse apply? What is the motivation for yielding to the other spouse's authority according to this verse? What about mutual submission?

11. One result of persistent bullheadedness is recorded in Proverbs 29:1 – a broken neck! What are other results that can be expected from a stubborn attitude that insists on its own way?

Thought Questions

12. Review the 4 termites that work on the sly to destroy marriages. Think about each one as it relates to your half of the marriage. Are there individual corrections you can make to improve your marriage? How do you feel about them as your sole responsibility, not your partner's?

13. Think again about the word submission. In the past, has it only been applied to the women in the house? Has this study changed that wrong conclusion? Apply "submitting to one another" to several household duties or tasks. Husbands, don't dodge this one! Are there some things your wife has mentioned again and again that needs your attention?

Putting It Into Practice

Make the following list of termites:
  Confusion in the Home
  Busyness that Runs Roughshod Over Others
  Insensitive to Anyone but Self
  Stubborn Attitudes that Don't Yield

Include this rating scale:
  Yes – It is a problem for 1 or more family members
  No – It is not a problem
  Maybe – It some day could be a problem

Have family members apply it to your home. Where are the danger areas? What can be done to shore up these weaknesses? Once again, husbands – how about setting a

34 date when you will follow through with your wife's requests? You will be amazed at how it affects her willingness to cooperate with you in some of your requests. Start soon!

7

HOW TO HAVE A GOOD FIGHT

Purposes

To surface some reasons why disagreements occur in marriage and to discover how a couple can maintain a proper attitude during times of conflict.

Scripture Input

1. Before you begin this section of questions about Scripture that relates to "good" fighting behavior, inventory your premarital understanding of one another. Did you know he liked TV sports? Did you know she liked to go to bed early and get up early? Did you know he was not handy with tools? Did you know she craves a clean house? Did you lead each other into thinking incorrectly about your likes and dislikes? Were you *really* honest?

Continue this probing of things you have discovered (or are yet to discover, if you aren't married) *since* the time that you were married. Have you had disagreements over these postmarital discoveries? Did the "love is blind" syndrome blur your vision of these trouble spots? Have you admitted this to each other yet?

2. Honesty is the best policy. Ephesians 4:25 lays this truth on the line regarding our speech. Read Philippinas 4:8. Notice the first 3 adjectives. Where does honesty begin? Will honest actions stem from honest thoughts? Paraphrase your own rule about thinking and speaking in honesty during disagreements.

3. Can you be angry without sinning? That is the meaning of Ephesians 4:26. This is anger under control. The same emotion was resident in Jesus at the time He cleansed

36   the temple—notice Matthew 21:12-13. Talk about the ways that anger can be controlled in your disagreements.

4. What are some problems with out-of-control arguing? Relate Proverbs 18:14-19 to this situation. Are there some deep emotional scars your rage has caused in your marriage? Again, be honest.

5. A third rule for fighting involves timing. Ephesians 4:26-27 talks about the ceasing of arguments before they stretch to the next day. Read Ecclesiastes 3:1-8. Is there a time to engage in a dispute—rather than covering it over—and a time to refrain from debate? What are some times that are absolutely "out" in your marriage as far as heated discussions are concerned? What signals do you watch for in your mate which indicate that the time is inappropriate?

6. We have talked about honesty, proper control, and timing as rules for "good" fighting. Ephesians 4:28 gives us another. A negative command is followed by a positive encouragement. A similar use of words occurs in the next verse. In most cases, a negative prohibition in the Bible is followed by a positive counteraction. Does this characterize your criticism of your mate? Can you give positive suggestions for those negative appraisals you make of his/her actions? Why are you more critical than encouraging? Tough question . . . but it needs to be addressed.

7. Tact is the watchword of the fifth rule for fighting. Do you know how to say the needed word without offending? Meditate on Proverbs 15:1,2, and 4. Discuss the advantages of being tactful.

8. We are told to put away from us "all bitterness and wrath and anger and clamor and slander"—along with all *malice*. This word means a spiteful type of wickedness. When you combine bitterness through slander with malice, you've got a public defamation for sure. Is public criticism of your mate a problem for you? Do you often use sarcasm to cut him or her down? What is this verse saying to you?

9. Read Ephesians 4:32. Now look up Colossians 3:12-13. Write out a definition of forgiveness from these verses. Does Christ's forgiveness of you have any bearing on your attitude toward your mate after a fight?

10. What is suggested as the best way to stop a fight in *Strike the Original Match?* (See page 111 in the book.) Can you remember a recent fight when admitting your wrong did not end the conflict? Or have you tried this solution yet?

Thought Questions

11. Who is the winner in any heated fight? Can a fight occur without some scuffs and scrapes and cuts being inflicted on both contenders? Talk about this fact—that everyone's a loser in an unfair fight—in relation to your home struggles today. How can you disagree without assaulting your partner?

12. The tongue can inflict deadly wounds during fights, either by open destruction or cutting sarcasm. One excellent suggestion in *Strike the Original Match* is to eliminate the words "never" and "always" when referring to your mate's shortcomings. For instance, don't say "she always does so and so" or "he never does this." Are these a couple of vocabulary words you two need to delete from your disagreement dialogues? How about the word "divorce"? If there are some terms that are "off limits," agree to their removal together. Both partners must cooperate.

13. Ephesians 4:30 speaks of the empowerment for all the character changes needed in your fighting patterns. What are the ways in which you grieve the Holy Spirit, prevent Him from enabling Christ's life to shine through you, when you ignore the fighting rules that have been outlined? Try to be painfully specific.

Putting It Into Practice

Role play each of the seven rules for fighting. First act out the wrong responses—not being honest, not using proper control, using poor timing, etc. Then act out the right responses properly observing the rules. Have different family members act in roles other than their own, reacting the way they see Mom, Dad, brother, or sister behave. Use the dramatizations as the basis for further discussion about family disagreements. Be ready to laugh. When you see yourself acted out in someone else's skin . . . it can be hilarious! And terribly convicting.

8

'TIL DEBT
DO US
PART

Purposes

To educate couples about one of the most common havoc-wreakers in a marriage—the mismanagement of money. And hopefully, to offer some guidelines for a couple who wants to manage their finances well.

Scripture Input

Read Proverbs 11:1, 14:23, 15:27, 22:7, 23:4-5, 27:23-24; Ecclesiastes 5:10; Matthew 22:15-22; Luke 19:11-26; Romans 13:6-8; 2 Corinthians 9:6-8; 1 Timothy 6:8-10, 17-19. (Ever wonder why they say that the Lord has more to say about money than the topics of heaven and hell combined?)

1. Several wrong attitudes have been developed by Christians with regard to money. One of the first is that the money you put in the bank is yours, except for the tenth you set aside for God. What does Psalm 50:10-11 say about any material thing on the earth? Read Luke 19:11-13. The noble-man in the parable is the Lord, and notice His attitude toward those He leaves His money with. Whose money is in the servants' possession?

2. A second wrong attitude is akin to the first. In Luke 19:13, the nobleman says *"Do business* with this (money) until I come back." Should we distinguish between our business practices and the "Lord's work"? Should we operate with any less integrity at the office than we do in conducting church business? What does Colossians 3:23-24 say about whatever business practice in which you engage?

40   3. Verse 14 of Luke 19 shows the antagonistic attitude some citizens had toward their leader's input about their money affairs. Often, we would rather do business our way than God's way–it's more comfortable, using the habits we are accustomed to. Read Psalm 127:1 and James 4:13-17. Do each of these passages favor including God's leadership in business? Does this approach differ from yours?

        4. Note the reaction of the master to the profits made by his servants in Luke 19:16-18. Rather than seeing the making of profits through wise money handling as unspiritual, what does the master's reaction indicate about God's attitude toward wise stewardship? Look up 1 Corinthians 4:2, Titus 1:7, and 1 Peter 4:10. Is wise stewardship a debit or a credit on God's ledger? What's another reason for keeping current on the wise use of your money according to Luke 12:42-48?

        5. Some people believe God smiles on self-imposed poverty. The stories of Luke 19:19-22 and Matthew 25:24-30 should forever dispel that notion. After reading those sections of Scripture, talk about your neglect of wise stewardship that has been due to the belief: "having a little is more spiritual than having much." How much of that attitude is the result of just plain laziness?

        6. Discipline is a requirement for any wise steward. Even the discipline to put money into savings is cited as more worthy than dumping it into a checking account according to Luke 19:23. Let's take a lesson on discipline from our friends the ants, here. Read Proverbs 6:6-8. Now that's using foresight and discipline! Should discipline be incorporated into your money affairs? In what ways?

        7. Some say the rich get richer and the poor get poorer. How does Luke 19:24-26 qualify that statement?

        8. Study the figure which details the peaks and valleys of earning on page 127 of Strike the Original Match. How many years do you have left to plan your investments? Have your children been informed–if they are old enough–of your plans? Have you shared wise management principles with them? Are you working with them in practical ways so they are putting these principles to work right now?

9. As you read Matthew 22:15-21, spell out the implica- **41** tions of Jesus' quick statements. Are you as purposeful in your giving to God as you are in your giving to government? Mentally compare the way you prepare your taxes and the way you determine your year's giving to the Lord. Which do you spend more time with? Which contribution will go further—eternally?

10. In Romans 13:8, the admonition is given to not be continually in debt to someone else. See if the following verses contain advice for your credit buying: Nehemiah 5:1-5; Proverbs 22:26; Matthew 18:25. This may hurt: Are you abusing your use of credit buying? Why?

11. A proper perspective on use of money is given in 1 Timothy 6:8-10, 17-19. Is money in and of itself evil? If the proper attitude toward money is maintained, what avenues of service open up to those with wealth? Look up Acts 20:35. Compare this well-known quote with 1 Timothy 6:17-19.

Thought Questions

12. Think about the four suggested guidelines for financial planning: Christ and Ceasar are essential, not optional; buying and borrowing demand short accounts; savings and security require planning; things and treasures are temporal. Translate each principle into a current family project. Engage your family in those projects.

13. Look at the suggested "10-70-20" plan included in *Strike the Original Match* on page 131. Calculate your budget—taking taxes and tithes first—according to this formula. How do you come out on the scale? Any plans to start some needed changes?

Putting It Into Practice

Debate each of the seven attitudes below in your home or couples' study. Have one pro voice and one con voice. (1) That part is God's . . . this part is mine. (2) God isn't concerned with secular things. (3) Let's not get fanatical! Leave God at church. (4) Success is suspect . . . profit-making is unspiritual. (5) Having little is more spiritual than having much. (6) Ignorance is bliss. Some day our ship will come in. (7) God isn't fair. The rich get richer and the poor get poorer.

42   Talk with your mate about struggles you've had with one or more of these attitudes. If it's necessary, seek the forgiveness of your partner for your failure with money management. If your partner has been disciplined and wise (occasionally without your support), *thank* your mate for being a consistent model.

DIVORCE: WHEN IT ALL COMES TUMBLING DOWN

Purposes

To understand and pursue solutions for the one problem that mars God's original blueprint for marriage—divorce.

Scripture Input

Read Genesis 5:1-3; Psalm 103:10-12; Matthew 19:3-9; 1 Corinthians 7:12-15, 39; 2 Corinthians 5:17; Ephesians 2:1-7, 19-27.

1. The picture of the original marriage was one of sinless happiness. But with the first sinful act of disobedience that was performed, what happened to the marriage that had been open before God? Read Genesis 3:1-15. How did this affect future marriages, as well as the state of man and woman individually? Compare Genesis 5:1-3 and Romans 5:12. How does the encroachment of sin affect man's attitude toward divorce? Matthew 19:8 will help you determine the answer.

2. Before we go further with biblical teaching on divorce, let's lay the groundwork for understanding what a marriage is. What actually constitutes a marriage?
    a. consent of the 2 partners
    b. leaving the respective homes
    c. a ceremony
    d. sexual intercourse
    e. any of the above
    f. all of the above
    g. none of the above

44   3. Look up the following verses as they relate to a marriage union: Matthew 19:4; Genesis 2:24; and Genesis 2:18. Look for the characteristics of monogamy, permanency, intimacy, and completion.

4. What are some biblical reasons for the institution of marriage? See Genesis 1:27,28; 1 Corinthians 7:2-5,9; and the Song of Solomon.

5. If the above questions give us the biblical understanding of what marriage is, then let's look at the possible reasons for the dissolution of that bond. Do the biblical grounds for marriage apply to non-Christians? Laying aside the conventions of our society, what reasons does the non-Christian have for adhering to biblical principles here? Then if two non-Christians do get a divorce, do biblical restrictions concerning divorce apply to them? (This is certainly not meant to encourage non-Christian couples to divorce; it simply points out how illogical it is to hold the non-believers to scriptural behavior patterns when they don't believe in God in the first place.) Think deeply about this before you answer.

6. With the above questions in mind, is a divorce between two non-believers restricted by the Bible? What should our response be to those who have experienced divorce before conversion? Read two Corinthians 5:17; Ephesians 2:1-7, 19-22; and Psalm 103:10-12. Dwell on what *God's* attitude (not your attitude) is toward those who have sinned—especially in the area of divorce—before they became Christians?

7. Read Matthew 19:3-9. What is the exception for divorce that Jesus states in this passage? Compare this also with Matthew 5:27-32. Note, too, that similar passages (Mark 10:2-12 and Luke 16:18) do not mention adultery's effect on marriage—seemingly allowing this exception to stand.

8. Even though this exception is given in Matthew, does this statement by Christ automatically necessitate divorce when immorality has occurred in a marriage? Remember the verses on forgiveness in the last question. How do these apply to a partner who temporarily strays in his fidelity? What does Jesus say about forgiveness in Matthew 18:21-22? Is forgiveness the better option than divorce when immorality occurs in a marriage? Again, think deeply before answering.

9. Study 1 Corinthians 7:12-15, 39. The overriding   45
emphasis in this passage is obviously to remain in marriage.
Even if one mate is not a Christian. However, what is per-
mitted if a non-Christian permanently deserts his mate? Who
initiates the action of leaving?

10. In verse 39, the bond of marriage is said to be broken
by the death of one partner and there is freedom to remarry.
Relate this to the freedom from "bondage" spoken of in
1 Corinthians 7:15 when a desertion occurs.

11. Do Paul's statements in 1 Corinthians 7:12-15 con-
tradict Jesus' words in Matthew 19, seeing that Jesus cited
only one exception? Did Jesus' audience differ from that of
Paul's? Was Jesus confronting the situation of a marriage
between a believer and a non-believer?

12. Back up to the verses before 1 Corinthians 7:12-15.
What is Paul's main thought here? Were the passages about
divorce written to provide ways for divorce to occur or were
they written to allow for the infections of sin that poison marriage? What is God's ideal for marriage?

13. Is divorce between two Christians who operate on
the true basis of love and forgiveness and follow God's will
ever really an option?

Thought Questions

14. What if two Christians desire to leave one another
because they simply can't get along? Is this grounds for
divorce? Are there times when a temporary separation might
be necessary? If so, name an example or two.

15. If a Christian desires reconciliation with his partner,
but the partner won't respond (even though he or she is a
Christian), what options are open to the one desiring reconciliation? Can he or she remarry?

16. Has divorce become "the unpardonable sin"?

17. Does the statement "because of the hardness of your
heart" have meaning today?

18. If divorce before conversion is no different than
Christian divorce, how do we counsel people who have ruined
their marriage already?

19. Is each divorce case to be considered individually?

20. What effect does a divorce have on a person who desires to serve in a church office? Does this situation prevent certain places of service from being open to him/her?

21. How does the teaching of grace apply to divorce? Be *very* careful here. Be certain that it is grace you are considering and not human license.

22. What other issues grow out of divorce?

Putting It Into Practice

Take a poll of friends and neighbors to determine what the average person on the street thinks about taking the problem of divorce to a church body or group of Christians. Do they sense that they would find acceptance or rejection? Are their expectations of Christian reactions warranted or not? How could these negative attitudes be corrected?

10

COMMITMENT IS THE KEY

Purpose

To encourage the one characteristic in a marriage union that can make it work—forever.

Scripture Input

Read Ecclesiastes 5:4, 8:11; Deuteronomy 6:10-15a; Ezekiel 33:30-33; Psalm 56:1-6, 9-11; 1 Corinthians 5:1-7, 6:9-10, 7:3-4, 10-13, 24-35.

1. The message in Ecclesiastes 5:4-5 is very clear: A vow or an oath is a promise that is meant to be kept. Does a marriage vow carry the force of this vow mentioned in Ecclesiastes? Why or why not?

2. Commitment is an old-fashioned word. It is an old-fashioned word that has been watered down by all the public opinion that has washed over it. An erosion has occured. Moses and the children of Israel faced antagonistic attitudes that were contrary to the plans God had spelled out for them. Read Deuteronomy 6:10-15a. Paul faced a similar problem and wrote 2 Timothy 4:3-4. What did you learn about public opinion in these two sections of Scripture? What is the more trustworthy source for determining your life?

3. Another force that weakens commitment is the tendency to ignore biblical principles and twist doctrinal truth into a more comfortable theology. Ezekiel 33:30-33 depicts a group of people who let their experience block out the truth. Notice verse 31—"(they) hear your words, but they do not do them." What principles of avoiding error-filled theology can be gleaned from the following sections of Scrip-

48 ture? Matthew 15:9; Romans 16:17,18; 2 Corinthians 2:17, 11:13; Ephesians 4:14; Colossians 2:4,8; 1 Timothy 6:3,4; 2 Peter 2:18-19.

4. Commitment can be weakened by our exploitation of God's grace! Because God delays the consequences of sin, many disobey and chuck commitment because they see no immediate bad effects. They accommodate their theology by their experience. Read Ecclesiastes 8:11. Now open your Bible to Psalm 37. Translate the message of the Psalm (the wicked will eventually get their just reward) into your own words. Note especially verses 7-9, 35-36.

5. Lastly, commitment can be weakened by Christian approval of its absence. Paul faced a problem of this scope at the church at Corinth, when a sinful brother had been embraced by fellow Christians and told that "Everything was all right." Hence, 1 Corinthians 5:1-7. What were the consequences for the sinful brother when discipline was finally instituted? What were the consequences for the church outlined by Paul?

6. On the realistic side, could a spouse's actions ever become so violent (due to emotional sickness or gross demonstrations of sin) that a temporary separation should be considered? Read Psalm 56 and underline the promises given by God for such a crisis time.

7. There are certain realizations which can enhance commitment to your mate. In 1 Corinthians 7:28, 32-35, one discoveres a sad, but true, observation about married life: No marriage is conflict-free or distraction-free. But here's the good news. Not one of those conflicts or distractions is insurmountable with Christ. What kind of a picture do the following verses give a Christian about his battles? Matthew 12:20; 1 Corinthians 15:54, 55, 57; 2 Corinthians 2:14; 1 John 5:4.

8. Another realization that aids the commitment factor is that working through a problem, rather than walking out, is God's way of solving any marital difficulty. The general tenor of 1 Corinthians 7:10-13, 24, and 27 is "Hang in there!" It's just like the posters that encourage, "Keep on Truckin!" Take a moment to list the consequences of divorce—the results of walking out—for the husband, the wife, *and* . . . the children. Is it really worth the pain it creates?

9. We have looked at 1 Corinthians 7:3-4 before as a model of unselfishness in marriage. A third realization that cements the commitment bond is to understand that commitment is not a matter of demanding rights . . . but releasing rights. What can we learn from Jesus' attitude of giving up His right to live in Matthew 26:42? How can we apply this attitude of giving up our own rights in marriage? If your marriage is shaky, try hard to be objective and not defensive here.

10. Being committed in marriage glorifies God because it says "God's way is best!" See 1 Corinthians 6:19-20. Think about how your marriage is or is not an example of the Ephesians 5 analogy. Are you glorifying God? Is that, genuinely, the bottom line goal of your life . . . your marriage . . . your commitment?

Thought Questions

11. Do a research project on commitment. Have every group member read an avant-garde magazine article about new approaches to marriage. Critique each author's input on how close he adheres to principles that either help or hinder commitment in marriage.

12. Talk with your spouse about making commitment a conscious part of your marriage. What attitudes need renovation or strengthening?

Putting It Into Practice

Write out your commitment to your mate in wording that is similar to wedding vows. Make it as eternal and lasting in tone as you possibly can. Take a quiet time this week to sit down with one another, and declare these vows face to face. Set up a periodic appointment for this practice, perhaps on your birthdays and at your anniversary each year.

NOTE: Consider having your "vow to commitment" printed nicely and possibly framed. Put it on the dresser in your bedroom or in your wedding album.

11

DON'T JUST GET OLDER, GET BETTER!

Purpose

To take a look at growing older from God's perspective and realize the opportunities out in front for married couples who don't want the pasture after sixty-five!

Scripture Input

Read Ecclesiastes 11:1-8, 12:1-7.

1. What do the following scriptures teach you about old age and those who are in the later years of life? Exodus 20:12; Leviticus 19:32; Job 12:12; Psalm 71:18, 92:12-14; Proverbs 16:31; 1 Timothy 5:1,2.

2. Is old age always to be equated with wisdom? Are older people always wiser and more mature in their judgment? In the book of Job, a scene takes place which shows that age does not always mean maturity. A younger man, Elihu, has to counsel his seniors as to their poor "bedside manner" with the ailing Job. This is the setting of Job 32:4-9 (please read). What can an older person learn from this scenario? When is a person "mature?" Relate these insights to fulfillment as an older married couple.

3. After you read Ecclesiastes 12:1-2, put these verses in your own words and on your own level. What is the warning being stated here? What else besides bitterness can make the last years of one's life a sad debacle, so sad that one says "I have no delight in them?"

4. List the physical problems of old age that are being described in Ecclesiastes 12:3-4a, 5b, 6b, 7. Do you get the feeling that a clock is grinding down to a halt? Can you add to this list of physical problems?

5. List the mental and emotional problems being described in Ecclesiastes 12:4b, 5a, and 6a as they relate to old age. Have you been to a rest home lately? Spotted any of these symptoms?

6. Where in the Bible can one find support for any of the many television commercials that spurn getting older and laud all sorts of fountain-of-youth tactics? What happens to those who attempt to dodge the reality of their age and inappropriately attempt to look twenty years younger than they really are? Do they hurt more than just themselves?

7. What can a mate do to help his or her partner face the realities of advancing age?

8. Besides facing reality, another guideline to help you get better as you grow older is to give generously. Read Ecclesiastes 11:1-2 in *The Living Bible* as well as in a standard translation. What does God say about generosity? Check 2 Corinthians 9:7-8 and Hebrews 6:10. What does Luke 12:16-21 say to those of us who are getting older?

9. What else can an older couple give besides money? As you read Ecclesiastes 11:1-2, think about the gifts of your time and your experience that can be shared with those younger than you. Now read Romans 12:13 and list some more ways of giving.

10. Ecclesiastes 11:3-4 tells about one who is actually letting life pass him or her by—he has set his mind that the back forty of his life will lie fallow, he will not reap or sow. If you apply 2 Corinthians 9:6 to planning for your future (as well as to giving), what does the Bible say that little planning will yield? What about a *lot* of planning?

11. The picture of Ecclesiastes 11:5-6 is a simple one: The only real security in life is that which is found in trusting God. Compare Proverbs 3:1-2, 9:11, and 10:27 with the Ecclesiastes section. What truths are evident?

12. The final word for getting better as you grow older is to rejoice in that reality—Ecclesiastes 11:7-8. What positives are added to the biblical perspective of rejoicing with the advent of old age when one adds 1 Thessalonians 5:18 to the picture? How is this life view different from Solomon's?

Thought Questions

13. When do you think you'll be too old to enjoy life? What Scripture will support you at that point and confirm that old age is another *good* part of God's life?

14. Take the 5-fold prescription given for getting better as you get older—live realistically, give generously, adapt willingly, trust fearlessly, rejoice daily. How will this change your attitude toward life today? By the way, take a long look at your face in a mirror. Is there a permanent crease in your forehead? Has a frown replaced that smile on your face? If so ask yourself *why*. Ask God to lighten your life with a renewed zest for living.

Putting It Into Practice

Arm yourself with this prescription for getting better with increased age, and select someone in your extended family to share the message with this week. Plan a field trip for your couples' group to a rest home—help someone's perspective on life as an older person to grow and get better.

12

WHAT TO DO WITH AN EMPTY NEST

and Conclusion

Purpose

To take one more look at marriage in later years and summarize our findings about marriage for the Christian.

Scripture Input

Read Proverbs 24:3-4; James 1:5, 3:17.

1. Look at the stages of marriage suggested on pages 183-184 of *Strike the Original Match.* Where are you? Which stage do your fear the most? Why?

2. What is an "emply nest?" How can a group of couples in this same stage of life band together to support one another?

3. The first empty-nest adjustment is said to be decreasing physical attractiveness. For the perceptive Christian woman (and man), how does Proverbs 31:30 apply to this situation?

4. Selfishness is a second hazard of the empty nest. Check the following scriptures and see how they apply to this problem: Romans 12:10, 15:1-3; 1 Corinthians 10:24, 13:4-5; Philippians 2:3,4.

5. Boredom, depression, and loneliness are three somewhat related problems of the empty nest. Stop and brainstorm right now about ways these dead-end avenues can be avoided as you get older. Are the solutions really tied to retirement monies or to retirement attitudes?

6. Divorce is seen as another adjustment that can droop the sails of any empty-nested couple. Does the presence of children in your home right now add to the cohesiveness of your marriage? What kind of glue would your marriage have if the children were suddenly gone?

7. Meditate on Proverbs 24:3-4 once again. Formulate your own definition of wisdom. How does it square with James's definition (1:5, 3:17)? How can it be employed to help avoid empty-nest struggles in your marriage? Get specific.

8. Refer back to the studies in chapters 1 and 2 on exercising wisdom, employing understanding, and applying knowledge. How can each of these different guidelines help construct a solid foundation for your marriage?

Thought Questions

9. What new thoughts do you have about God's divine blueprint for marriage that have been gleaned from the study of *Strike the Original Match?* In what areas is your marriage stronger? In what areas is it still weak?

10. Compare the popular song in the book's introduction (pages 10-11) with the poem recorded in the book's conclusion (pages 195-196). Are there similarities between the two pieces? Are there differences? If there are differences, what accounts for them? Does either the song or the poem express the desire to go on in marriage? Although the song and the poem express the negative side, what gives us hope as we follow the blueprint for the original match?

Putting It Into Practice

Make plans right now for a committed prayer group composed of friends you have made in your couples' study. Commit yourselves to a once-a-month gathering for support, strength, and encouragement of strong, healthy marriages.

Scripture Index

Subject Index